S0-BYO-255

Amazing Animals

This edition first published in MMXVIII by
Book House

Distributed by Black Rabbit Books
P.O. Box 3263
Mankato, Minnesota 56002

© MMXVIII The Salariya Book Company Ltd
All rights reserved.
No part of this book may be reproduced, stored
in a retrieval system or transmitted in any
form or by any means, electronic, mechanical,
photocopying, recording or otherwise, without
the written permission of the copyright owner

Cataloging-in-Publication Data is available
from the Library of Congress

Printed in the United States
At Corporate Graphics,
North Mankato, Minnesota

9 8 7 6 5 4 3 2 1

ISBN: 978-1-911242-70-3

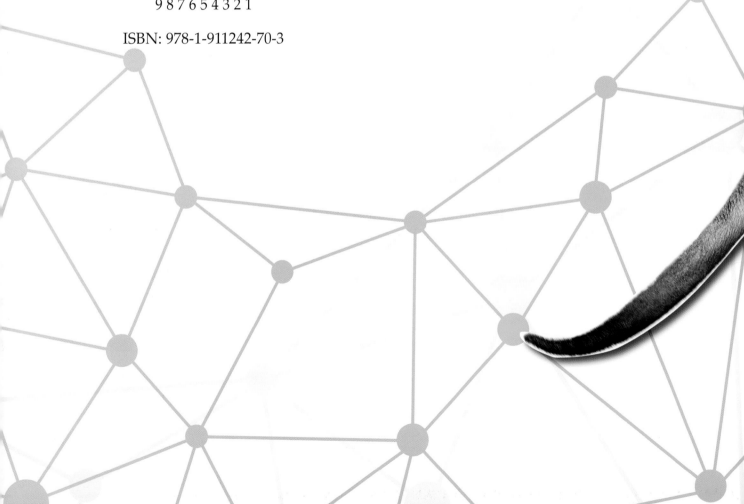

ZAP!

Amazing Animals

Richard & Louise Spilsbury

Contents

The flying squirrel moves its tail to steer. The tail is used like a brake to help it to stop when it reaches its destination.

Why Animals Are Amazing

The blood vessels in a fennec fox's ears easily lose heat to the air. This helps the fox stay cool.

There are millions of different types of animals, including monkeys that are as small as a human finger and blue whales that have a heart the size of a small car. Most of these animals have amazing **adaptations** that make them perfectly suited to the **habitats** in which they live.

Animals have **evolved** these different features in order to survive, to find food or a mate, or to escape danger. For example, the fennec fox has giant ears that help to keep it cool so that it can survive in the hot desert.

Throughout this book, we will look at many other animals and the amazing features and behaviors they have to help them to survive.

The flying squirrel does not fly. It has stretchy membranes between its wrists and ankles that acts as a parachute, helping it to float from tree to tree. This floating helps it avoid predators on the forest floor.

Making an Elephant

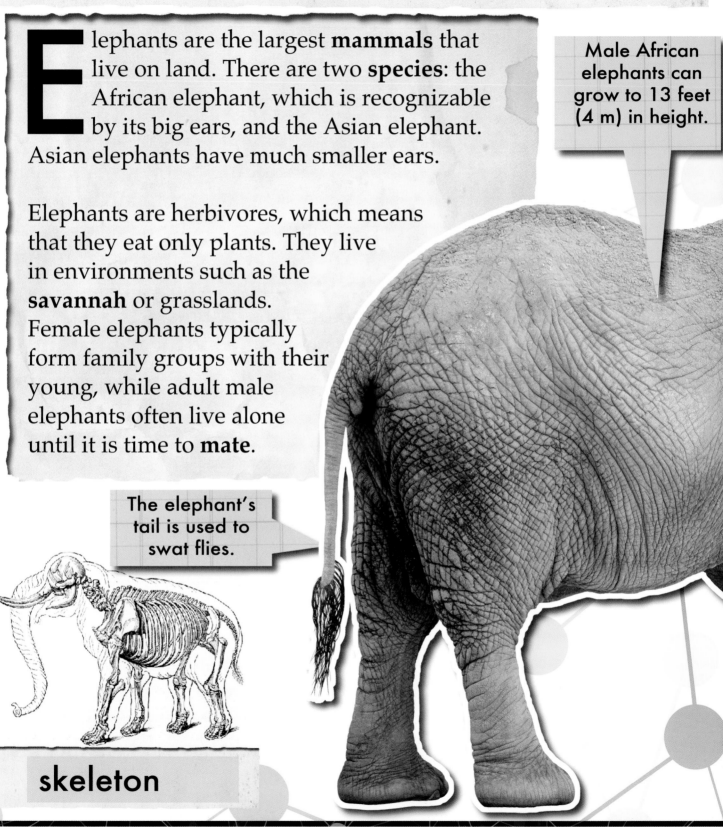

Elephants are the largest **mammals** that live on land. There are two **species**: the African elephant, which is recognizable by its big ears, and the Asian elephant. Asian elephants have much smaller ears.

Elephants are herbivores, which means that they eat only plants. They live in environments such as the **savannah** or grasslands. Female elephants typically form family groups with their young, while adult male elephants often live alone until it is time to **mate**.

Male African elephants can grow to 13 feet (4 m) in height.

The elephant's tail is used to swat flies.

skeleton

Elephants are one of the few species other than humans that can recognize themselves in a mirror.

Skin

An elephant's skin is usually gray and very thick. It can be an inch (2.5 cm) thick on the back and on parts of the head. To protect their skin from sunburn and mosquito bites, elephants spray themselves with mud.

Ingredients

- carbon (C)
- water (H2O)
- DNA

If you wanted to make an elephant, you would need to start with the **element** carbon. Carbon is the basis of all life on Earth. This is probably because carbon is exceptionally good at forming the long chemical bonds needed in a complex **organism** like an elephant. The **DNA** in each cell of an elephant contains the information that decides how it grows, how it behaves, and what it looks like.

Endangered Species

Both species of elephant are **endangered**. There are only around 40,000 to 50,000 Asian elephants and around 470,000 African elephants left in the wild. Since 1979, more than half of elephants' natural habitat has vanished. Elephants are also killed for their ivory tusks.

An African elephant can reach a speed of 25 miles per hour (40 kilometers per hour) when charging.

An elephant has a very good memory.

Hopping Kangaroos

Being able to hop along quickly means kangaroos can cover large distances in search of food and water, allowing them to thrive in the harsh, dry **climate** of the Australian outback. Kangaroos can hop faster than any other mammal.

Kangaroos have strong, elastic **tendons** in their legs that store energy for hopping. When a kangaroo's feet hit the ground, these tendons compress, much like a giant spring being pressed down. When the legs straighten again, the energy stored in the tendons pushes the kangaroo up into the air.

A kangaroo's tail is long, thick, and strong to help it balance and turn when it is hopping around.

A kangaroo's back legs and feet are big and strong to give it the power it needs to hop.

A kangaroo hops with both feet pushing off the ground at the same time because it cannot move its legs separately.

Kangaroos are the only large animals that move around by hopping.

Saving Energy

Jumping saves kangaroos energy. By bouncing along, they can go farther using less effort. At higher speeds, kangaroo hopping ranks among the most energy-efficient means of land travel in the animal kingdom.

Statistics

- Kangaroos can take single leaps that are up to 26 feet (8 m) long and 6 feet (1.8 m) high.

- Kangaroos can jump along at steady speeds of up to 35 miles per hour (56 km/h).

- Over short distances, kangaroos can race at up to 43 miles per hour (70 km/h).

Kangaroo mothers carry their babies in a pouch on their stomachs.

Competition from Fleas

For their size, fleas can jump higher than kangaroos. A tiny flea uses its long back legs to jump 130 times its own height. That is like a human leaping over the Eiffel Tower in Paris, France.

Kangaroos also sit back on their tails for support when they rest.

Intelligent Ants

A single ant is not too bright, but together, a **colony** of ants is incredibly smart. A colony is much like a brain in which there are many **neurons**. A single neuron does something simple but the whole brain can make many decisions.

No one ant is a leader. The queen ant is not the colony's ruler. She just lays all the eggs. Ants communicate constantly by releasing and sensing chemical signals called **pheromones**. These help other ants follow a trail, protect their nests, and form life rafts if there is a flood.

Ants on the Move

Pheromones help ants move as one. If there are two routes to find food, groups of ants start by taking both routes. Ants taking the shorter route travel faster, so the amount of pheromones on that route grows faster. Soon, more ants use that shorter route.

Farmers

Ants and human beings are the only animals that farm other creatures. Ants collect and care for aphid eggs and keep the aphids that hatch. The ants feed on the sweet honeydew that aphids release when groomed.

Protecting the Nest

Ants also combine their brain power to keep the colony safe. Each ant learns to recognize a few predators so that together a colony can recognize many. When a **predator** is near, some ants recognize it and alert the others to attack.

An ant's brain allows it to remember, think, and react to its surroundings.

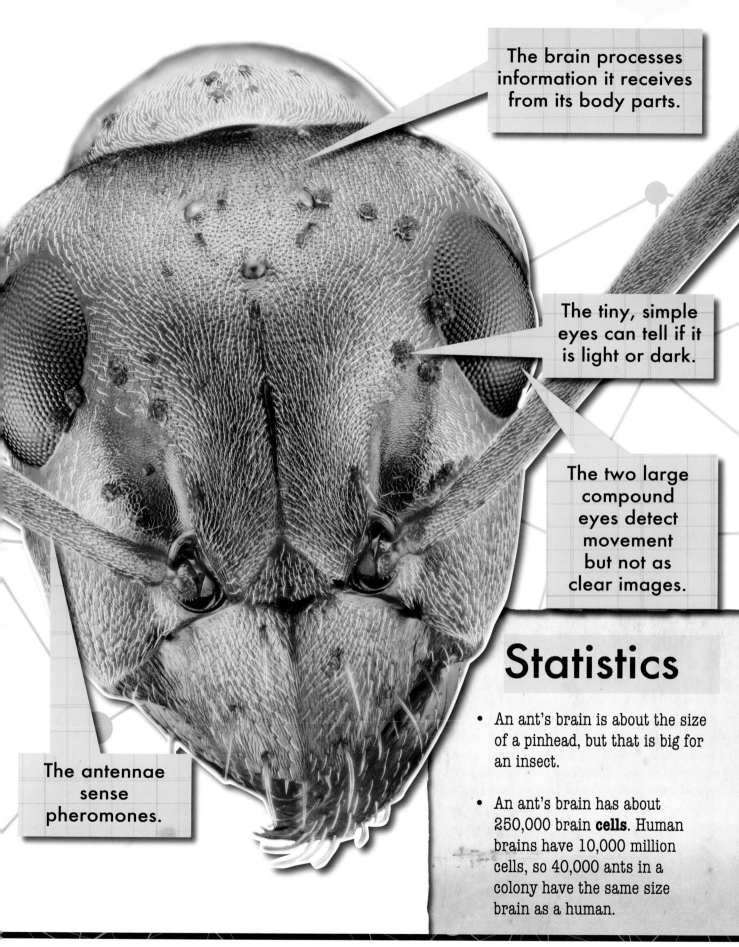

The brain processes information it receives from its body parts.

The tiny, simple eyes can tell if it is light or dark.

The two large compound eyes detect movement but not as clear images.

The antennae sense pheromones.

Statistics

- An ant's brain is about the size of a pinhead, but that is big for an insect.

- An ant's brain has about 250,000 brain **cells**. Human brains have 10,000 million cells, so 40,000 ants in a colony have the same size brain as a human.

Stunning
Sense of Smell

When people sniff the air, they suck small clouds of chemicals up their noses, which they sense as smell. Animals have different ways of "smelling" chemicals, and they use smell for different things.

Marking Territory

Hippopotamuses use dung to mark the territory where they and their large family live. The smell of their dung warns other hippos to keep away. Hippos spin their tails while **defecating**. This spreads their **excrement** over the widest possible area. In places that a hippo marks often, there can be piles of dung up to 20 inches (50 cm) deep.

Recognition

A ewe instantly bonds with her newborn lamb. She can tell it apart from other lambs by its unique scent. This smell bond is so strong that a ewe will not accept a lamb that smells different from her own. If her lamb dies, a farmer may try wrapping its dead skin around an orphan lamb to persuade the ewe to adopt and feed it.

Great white sharks can detect a single drop of blood in 10 billion drops of water.

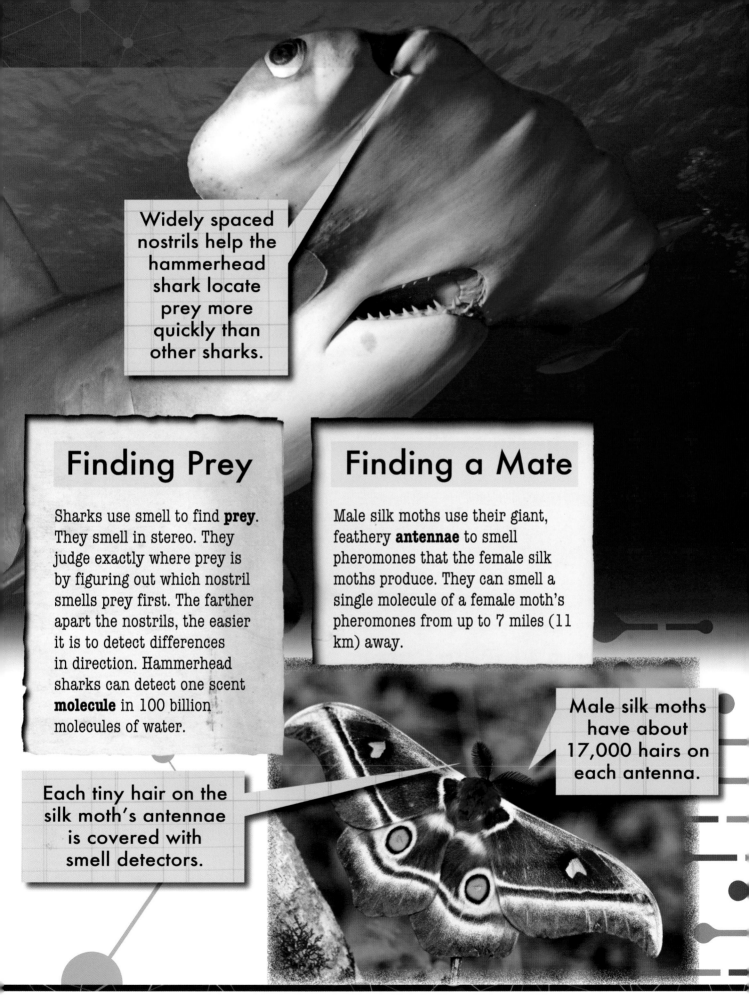

Widely spaced nostrils help the hammerhead shark locate prey more quickly than other sharks.

Finding Prey

Sharks use smell to find **prey**. They smell in stereo. They judge exactly where prey is by figuring out which nostril smells prey first. The farther apart the nostrils, the easier it is to detect differences in direction. Hammerhead sharks can detect one scent **molecule** in 100 billion molecules of water.

Finding a Mate

Male silk moths use their giant, feathery **antennae** to smell pheromones that the female silk moths produce. They can smell a single molecule of a female moth's pheromones from up to 7 miles (11 km) away.

Male silk moths have about 17,000 hairs on each antenna.

Each tiny hair on the silk moth's antennae is covered with smell detectors.

Silk moth antennae are large and wide to catch as many pheromone molecules as possible.

Creatures of the Deep

Life underwater is challenging. Animals that live underwater have to get oxygen, move through dense water that slows them down, and see in pitch blackness.

Deep-water animals also have to cope with the **pressure** exerted by the weight of the water above them. At 328 feet (1,000 m) down, an animal experiences 100 times the pressure it does at the surface.

The sperm whale's **streamlined** shape reduces **drag**, so it moves through water more easily.

Breathing Underwater

As fish swim along, water passes through special body parts on their sides called gill slits. Oxygen dissolved in seawater passes into blood vessels in the gills so fish can breathe underwater. Whales and dolphins are mammals, so they have to come to the surface to breathe.

Adult sperm whales can grow up to 66 feet (20 m) long.

Deep Diving

Sperm whales hunt squid that live in very deep water. To survive the water pressure this deep in the ocean, the sperm whale's rib cage folds and collapses, and the lungs compress to 1 percent of their size at the surface.

The sperm whale can dive down to a depth of about 6,500 feet (2,000 m).

Bioluminescence

Bioluminescence is the ability to produce light. Jellyfish produce light almost like a burglar alarm—to scare off predators. In jellyfish, a chemical reaction takes place when molecules of a substance called luciferin react with oxygen to produce light.

Flashing lights can be a good deterrent in the deep, dark ocean.

Ups and Downs

Most fish have a gas-filled sac called a swim bladder inside their bodies, just below their backbones. The swim bladder fills with air to help fish rise. It also releases air so that fish can sink.

Sperm whales can stay underwater for about an hour at a time.

Incredible Invisibility

Animals do not become invisible, but some use colors, patterns, or body shapes that blend into their surroundings, so they seem to disappear.

An octopus has thousands of chromatophores just below the skin to make it invisible.

Master of Disguise

An octopus can change color to match its surroundings using cells called chromatophores. Each one contains a tiny sac of black, brown, orange, red, or yellow **pigments**. To match a brown surface, for example, the brown sacs expand and the others contract, making the octopus look brown.

Seasonal Changes

The mountain hare's brown-gray coat **molts** in summer, and the hare grows white fur for the winter. The coat changes back to brown-gray again the following summer. Changing color provides the hares with **camouflage** against snow in winter and soil and rocks in summer.

If its camouflage fails, an octopus escapes by squirting a cloud of ink to confuse its predators.

Warning Colors

Some animals are colored to be more visible. Poison dart frogs are brightly colored with a range of strong patterns. Their colors send a clear signal to would-be predators to avoid them, if they want to live.

A poison dart frog's bright colors show up well in the shadowy rain forest.

Stick or Insect?

Stick insects are long-bodied insects that look just like twigs. Some even have flaps on their bodies that look like leaves. They keep still or sway in the wind, like the twigs they sit on, to hide from predators, such as birds.

Poison dart frogs keep their poison in glands beneath their skin.

A golden poison dart frog contains enough poison to kill ten adult humans!

Fantastic Flying Animals

A bird gets up into the air by flapping its wings. Flapping its wings downward pushes air down and the bird up. On the upward stroke, the bird folds in its wings, to avoid pushing air back up again.

In the air, birds can glide along because the curved shape of their wings creates a force called lift. Lift is an upward pushing force that comes from the air.

When hummingbirds hover, their wings move in a figure–eight pattern.

Lift

Air blowing over the top of a curved wing has farther to go, so it travels faster than the air below the wing. That means it has less time to push downward on the wing.

Air below the wing has more pushing power than air above, so it pushes the wing upward.

Hummingbirds flap, or beat, their wings up to 200 times per second.

Built for Flight

Birds have several features that help them fly:
- They have strong chest muscles to flap their wings.
- They have smooth, lightweight feathers to reduce the forces of weight and drag.
- They have hollow bones with air sacs inside them to make them light and thin and tiny cross pieces inside to make them strong.
- They have streamlined bodies to help reduce drag.

Hummingbirds get their name from the humming sound their fast-beating wings make.

Record Breaker

The Alpine swift can fly for six months nonstop when it **migrates** from Europe to Africa for the winter. This bird feeds in the air, catching small insects and seeds blowing in the wind. It gets water from its food. To rest, it glides, rather than flaps, its wings.

Aerial Acrobat

Hummingbirds can hover in one spot, fly straight up like a helicopter, fly down, sideways, backward, and even upside down.

Hummingbirds are the only birds that can fly backward.

Seeing in the Dark

Bush babies, owls, and many other **nocturnal** animals have big eyes. Large eyes with a larger pupil, lens, and **retina** let in more light.

Nocturnal animals do not see in color, and their vision is a bit blurry. Their night vision allows them to see enough for them to hunt, feed, and survive in the dark.

Rods and Cones

Eyes contain two types of light-sensing cells: rods and cones. Cones sense color but need bright light to work. Rods sense dim and scattered light but do not pick up color. The retinas of nocturnal animals have many rods to help them see at night. They have few cones.

Turning Heads

Owls' eyes are tube-shaped, rather than spherical like humans' eyes. This means the eyes cannot turn in their sockets like humans' do. Instead, owls twist their heads almost 360 degrees to see all around.

An owl's eyes fill more than half of its skull.

In dim light, owls see up to 100 times better than humans.

The tapetum is what makes cats' eyes shine in the headlights of a car.

Cats' Eyes

Cats' eyes have a layer, called the tapetum, behind the retina, which works a bit like a mirror. When light passes through the retina, it reflects off the tapetum. This gives the retina a second chance to sense it.

Owl necks have twice as many **vertebrae** as a human neck.

Lions and Light

Lions hunt at night. As well as a tapetum and a lot of rod cells, these big cats have a white stripe under each eye that helps them to see. This stripe reflects a faint light into the eyes, increasing the amount of light entering the lion's eyes.

Cats' eyes have six to eight times more rod cells than human eyes.

Animals that Navigate

Some animals find their way using Earth's **magnetic field**. The iron-rich rocks at Earth's core create magnetic poles at the North and South Poles. Some animals can sense variations in the angle or strength of Earth's magnetic field to find their way.

Other animals, such as bats, navigate using echolocation. They send out sounds and listen to the echoes that bounce back to locate prey or obstacles.

Loggerhead sea turtles are named after their large heads.

Experts think that loggerhead sea turtles may have magnetic receptors in their heads.

Loggerhead sea turtles have powerful jaws so they can feed on hard-shelled prey.

Loggerhead Locations

After baby loggerhead sea turtles hatch from eggs on a beach, they swim around the world. Five to ten years later, adult females use Earth's magnetic field to swim back to the exact beach where they were born to lay their eggs.

Loggerhead Migration

Loggerhead sea turtles travel about 8,000 miles (12,900 km) clockwise around the Atlantic Ocean. They migrate to find plentiful shellfish to eat.

Bat Echolocation

Bats make calls as they fly. The echoes that come back give them information about anything that is ahead of them, including the size and shape of an insect and which way it is going.
A bat can tell how far away an insect is by the time it takes the echoes to return. Some bats make echolocation sounds by clicking their tongues.

Sound waves reflect back after hitting prey.

sound waves sent out by bat

Bat Facts

- Bats fly at night, so they use echolocation to "see" in the dark.
- Bats make sounds that are too high for most humans to hear naturally.
- Most bats emit sounds through their mouths, but some produce sounds through their nostrils.
- Bats are the only mammals that can fly.

Coping with a Snakebite

The secret to surviving a snakebite is to stay calm but move quickly. A snakebite victim should keep the part of the body that was bitten still while going to a hospital. He or she should tell doctors what the snake looked like so that they can give the correct medicine to stop the **venom** from working.

Fangs are sharp, hollow, or grooved teeth that are used to inject venom into the victim's bloodstream.

Snakes use venom to kill prey and for self-defense. Snakes are **cold-blooded**. They lie in the sun to become warm enough to function. Most people are bitten when they accidentally disturb a basking snake.

The fangs are connected to a small sac of venom in the snake's head.

When a snake loses or breaks a fang, it grows another one.

Snakes with really long fangs can fold them back into the mouth to avoid biting themselves.

How Venom Works

Venom works in different ways:

- Hemorrhagic venom causes uncontrollable bleeding, so animals bleed to death from the inside.

- Neurotoxic venom attacks the brain and **nervous system,** causing muscles, such as the heart, to stop working.

Making Antivenom

Antivenom is medicine to stop the symptoms of the venom. To make antivenom, a small, harmless amount of snake venom is injected into a large animal. The animal's **immune system** produces antibodies to stop the venom. Antibodies from the animal are used to make antivenom.

Constrictors

Nonvenomous snakes, like boa constrictors, squeeze prey to death. They quickly coil their flexible bodies round and round a victim. By tightening the coils, the snake stops its prey from breathing. A boa constrictor's jaws unhinge so it can open its mouth wide and swallow a large victim whole.

Snakes can bite and inject venom for more than an hour after they have died.

Creating a Wildlife Habitat

A good wildlife habitat should have everything animals need. Animals need food to eat, water to drink, shelter from bad weather and danger, and a safe place to have their young.

Having different habitats in an area encourages a range of animals. This is important because plants and animals in an **ecosystem** are interdependent. They rely on each other to survive.

Nectar-rich flowers provide food for bees, butterflies, and other insects.

Dead leaves and sticks provide a home for ladybugs and other invertebrates.

Beetles, centipedes, spiders, and wood lice live beneath decaying wood and bark.

A dead tree provides food for insects and nest sites for birds and bats.

An average garden could hold more than 2,000 different species of insect.

Pond Life

Creating a pond is a great way to help wildlife. A pond is a breeding place for frogs, toads, newts, and dragonflies. It provides drinking and bathing water for birds and other animals. Plants can add oxygen to the water.

A Wildlife Garden

A wildlife garden will bring many different animals to an area. Piles of fallen leaves and dead wood will encourage insects. Tall grass will provide shelter and a place for insects to lay eggs. Birds and other wildlife will feed on the insects once they are born. Flowers that have turned to seed will provide food for birds, too.

Bee Hotel

Solitary bees, unlike honeybees that live in hives, lay their eggs in tunnels in wood or soil. A bee hotel can be made by filling a box with different-sized hollow tubes. The hotel needs to be somewhere that is protected from the rain and in a sunny spot. It should be placed near flowers so the bees can collect nectar and pollen to feed their young.

Compost Heaps

Putting household waste into a compost heap helps the environment and wildlife, too. Slugs and snails, wood lice, millipedes, earwigs, worms, beetles, and other animals all feed on the decaying food waste, and these attract hedgehogs, birds, frogs, and toads that feed on them.

Some weeds, such as nettles, can support more than 40 species of insect.

Tracking
Wild Animals

Before people can identify animal tracks, they need to find them! They should look for animal runs or beds, hair caught on a bush, flattened grass, and disturbed leaves on the forest floor. It is better to search away from main paths and to look for prints in mud, soft dirt, or sand.

The best animal traces are footprints and droppings. To work out which animal left the traces, it is best to use an identification guide with detailed illustrations and descriptions.

Assessing Prints

Size: Smaller prints mean smaller animals.
Number of toes: Weasels have five toes on all feet. Cats have four front and back.
Claws: Cats pull in claws when walking. Dog and fox claws stay out.
Size of claws: Badger claws are much longer than dog and fox claws.
Different size prints: Rabbits and hares have small front feet and large back feet.

Dog or Fox?

What is the difference between fox and dog droppings? Fox scat, or droppings, are usually darker and have twisted ends. Fox scat also contains rabbit and rodent hair.

Dog paw prints are more spread out and rounded.

Fox paw prints are narrower and diamond-shaped.

Bird tracks are very thin because they walk on their toes, not their feet.

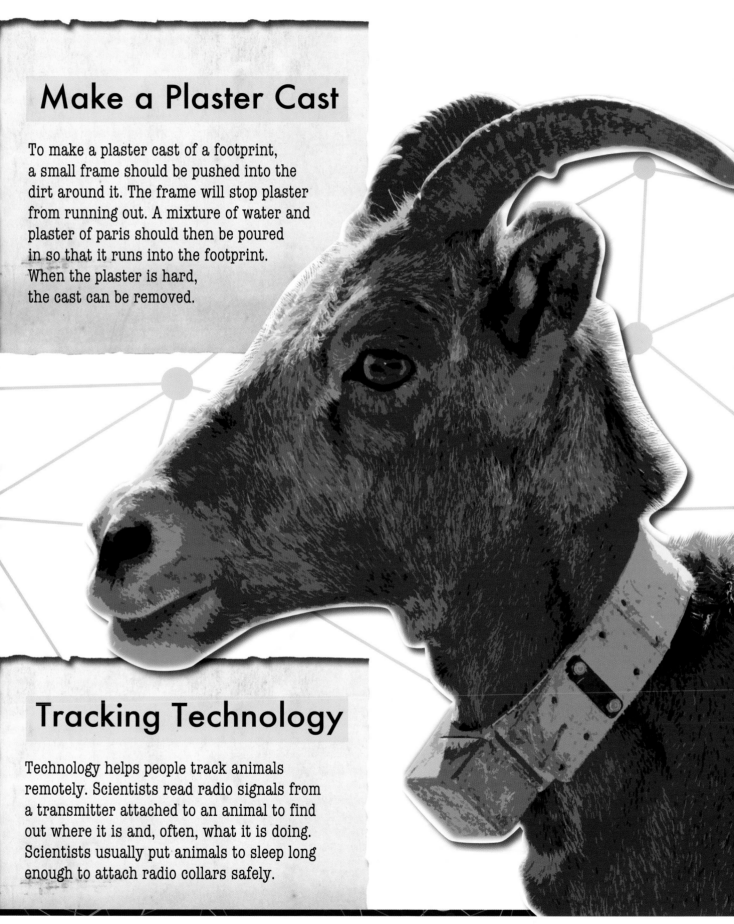

Make a Plaster Cast

To make a plaster cast of a footprint, a small frame should be pushed into the dirt around it. The frame will stop plaster from running out. A mixture of water and plaster of paris should then be poured in so that it runs into the footprint. When the plaster is hard, the cast can be removed.

Tracking Technology

Technology helps people track animals remotely. Scientists read radio signals from a transmitter attached to an animal to find out where it is and, often, what it is doing. Scientists usually put animals to sleep long enough to attach radio collars safely.

Fox dung can look whitish-gray in summer when it contains more animal bones.

Glossary

Adaptations Features or behaviors of a living thing that help it to survive.

Antennae Body parts found on an animal's head that are used to sense and feel things.

Camouflage Coloring or shape that allows something to blend in with its surroundings.

Cells Very small parts (or building blocks) that form all living things.

Climate The average weather conditions of a place.

Cold-blooded Having a body temperature that changes with the surroundings.

Colony A group of the same type of animal or plant living or growing together.

Defecating Getting rid of waste from the body.

DNA Deoxyribonucleic acid, which is the genetic material that determines the makeup of all living cells.

Drag The force of air pushing against something and slowing it down.

Ecosystem Everything that lives together in a particular habitat.

Element A substance that cannot be broken down into simpler substances by chemical means.

Endangered In danger of dying out or becoming extinct.

Evolved Changed and developed over a long period of time.

Excrement Feces or waste matter excreted from the body.

Habitats Environments in which an animal or plant normally lives or grows.

Immune system Parts of the body that protect it from diseases and infection.

Invertebrates Animals without backbones.

Magnetic field The invisible area around a magnet in which the force of magnetism acts.

Mammals Animals that usually have hair or fur and feed their young on their own milk.

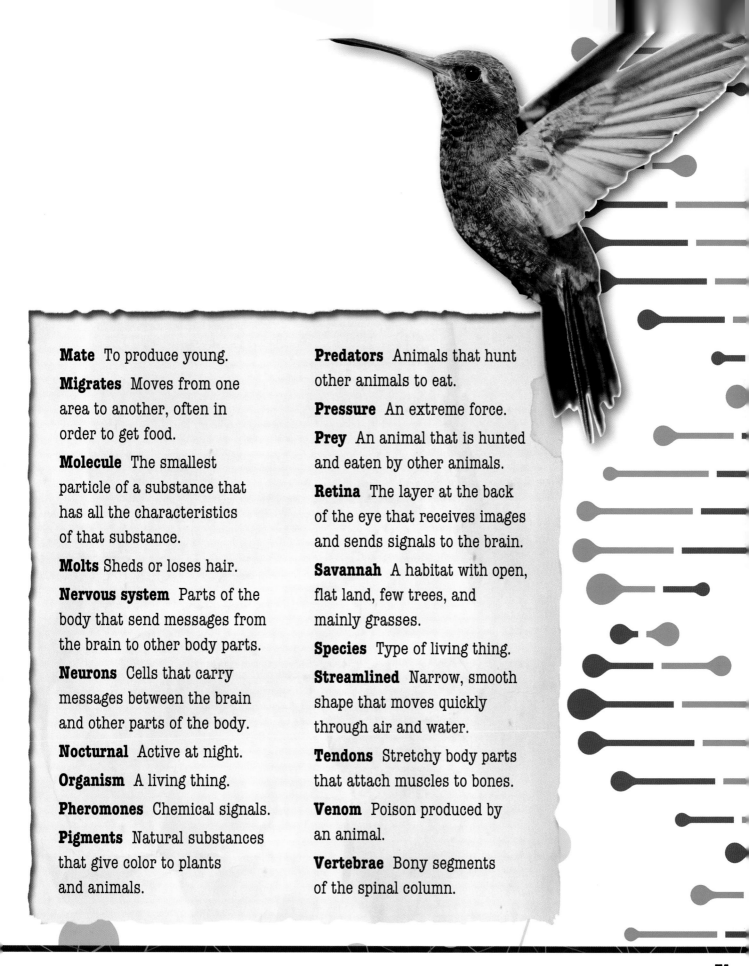

Mate To produce young.

Migrates Moves from one area to another, often in order to get food.

Molecule The smallest particle of a substance that has all the characteristics of that substance.

Molts Sheds or loses hair.

Nervous system Parts of the body that send messages from the brain to other body parts.

Neurons Cells that carry messages between the brain and other parts of the body.

Nocturnal Active at night.

Organism A living thing.

Pheromones Chemical signals.

Pigments Natural substances that give color to plants and animals.

Predators Animals that hunt other animals to eat.

Pressure An extreme force.

Prey An animal that is hunted and eaten by other animals.

Retina The layer at the back of the eye that receives images and sends signals to the brain.

Savannah A habitat with open, flat land, few trees, and mainly grasses.

Species Type of living thing.

Streamlined Narrow, smooth shape that moves quickly through air and water.

Tendons Stretchy body parts that attach muscles to bones.

Venom Poison produced by an animal.

Vertebrae Bony segments of the spinal column.

Index